ANIMALS
That Make a Difference!

Pigs

Ashley Lee

Explore other books at:
WWW.ENGAGEBOOKS.COM

VANCOUVER, B.C.

e↗ WWW.ENGAGEBOOKS.COM

Pigs: Level 1
Animals That Make a Difference!
Lee, Ashley 1995 –
Text © 2021 Engage Books

Edited by: A.R. Roumanis
and Lauren Dick

Text set in Arial Regular.
Chapter headings set in Arial Black.

FIRST EDITION / FIRST PRINTING

LIBRARY AND ARCHIVES CANADA CATALOGUING IN PUBLICATION

Title: Animals That Make a Difference: Pigs Level 1
Names: Lee, Ashley, author.

Identifiers: Canadiana (print) 20200309102 | Canadiana (ebook) 20200309110
ISBN 978-1-77437-682-9 (hardcover)
ISBN 978-1-77437-683-6 (softcover)
ISBN 978-1-77437-684-3 (pdf)
ISBN 978-1-77437-685-0 (epub)
ISBN 978-1-77437-686-7 (kindle)

Subjects:
LCSH: Swine—Juvenile literature
LCSH: Human-animal relationships—Juvenile literature

Classification: LCC SF395.5 .L44 2020 | DDC J636.4—DC23

Contents

What Are Pigs?

Pigs are animals with short legs and curly tails.

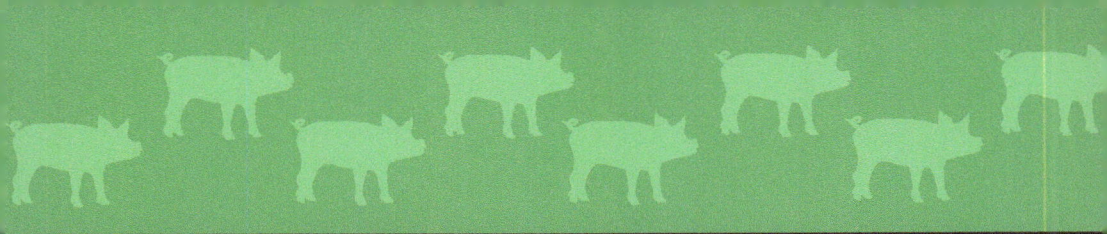

Pigs can be pink, black, or brown.

What Do Pigs Look Like?

Most pigs weigh between 300 and 700 pounds (140 and 300 kilograms).

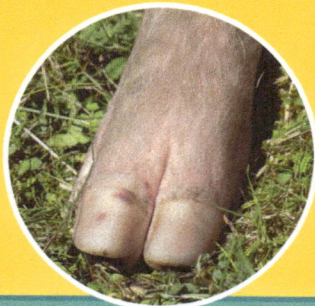

A pig's toes are covered by a hard nail.

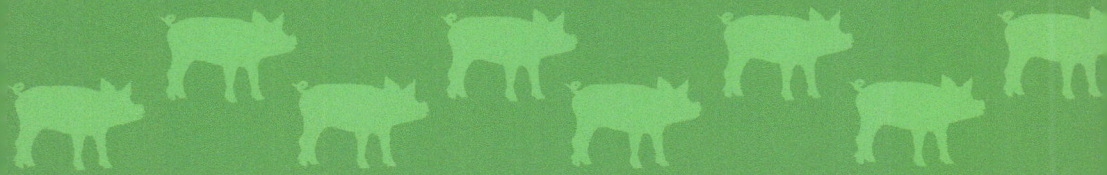

A pig's nose and upper lip is called a snout.

Wild pigs have long teeth called tusks.

Where Do Pigs Live?

Many pigs live on farms. Some pigs live in the wild.

Kunekune pigs come from New Zealand. Tamworth pigs come from England. Mukota pigs are mainly found in Zimbabwe.

Arctic
Ocean

England

Asia

New Zealand

Africa

Zimbabwe

Pacific
Ocean

Atlantic
Ocean

Australia

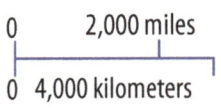

0   2,000 miles

0   4,000 kilometers

N

Legend
☐ Land
☐ Ocean

Southern
Ocean

Antarctica

9

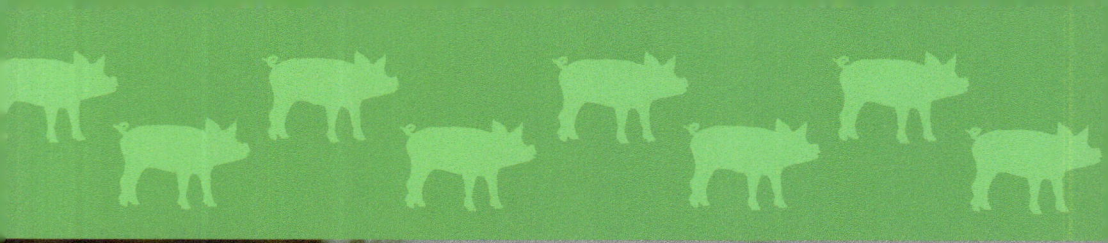

What Do Pigs Eat?

Pigs on farms mostly eat corn or grass.

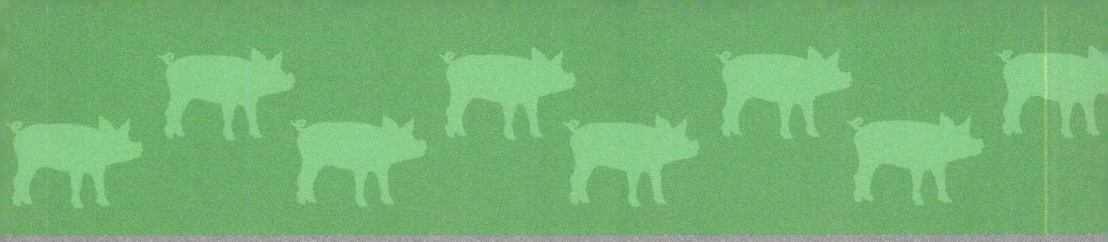

Wild pigs eat leaves, roots, and fruit.

How Do Pigs Talk to Each Other?

Pigs talk by grunting and moving their bodies. Pigs grunt over and over again when they want something.

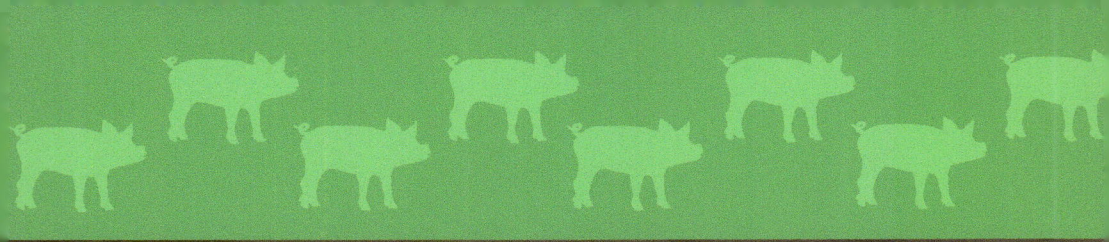

Happy pigs wag
their tails.

Pigs roll in
mud when
they want to
cool down.
This can also
mean they
want to play.

Pig Life Cycle

Pigs have about 10 babies at one time.

Baby pigs are called piglets.

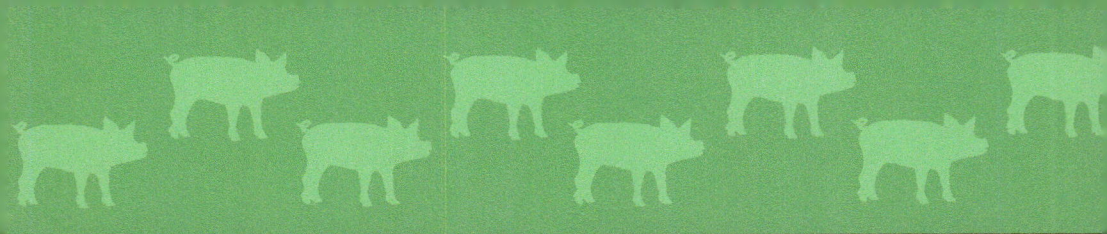

Pigs stop growing when they are between 2 and 3 years old.

Pigs live for 10 to 15 years.

Curious Facts About Pigs

Some people train pigs to find wild mushrooms called truffles.

Pigs are one of the smartest animals kept by people.

Mother pigs sing to their babies.

Pigs like to sleep
nose-to-nose
with their friends.

Pigs are
playful animals.
They rarely get
into fights.

Pigs have four
toes but they only
walk on two.

Kinds of Pigs

There are more than three hundred different kinds of pigs. About two billion pigs are kept by people. There are around seven million wild pigs.

Potbelly pigs have large stomachs.

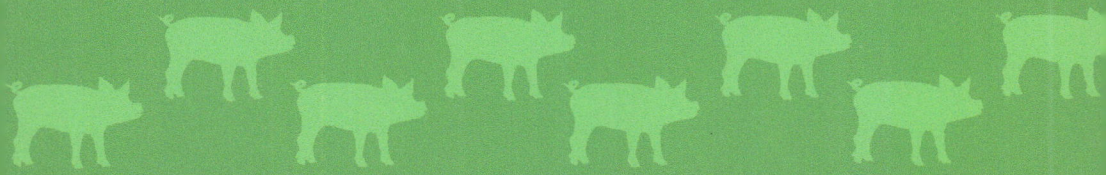

Mangalica pigs have thick, curly hair.

Red river hogs are red with a white stripe down their backs.

How Pigs Help Earth

Pigs dig up dirt with their noses.

This helps new plants grow.

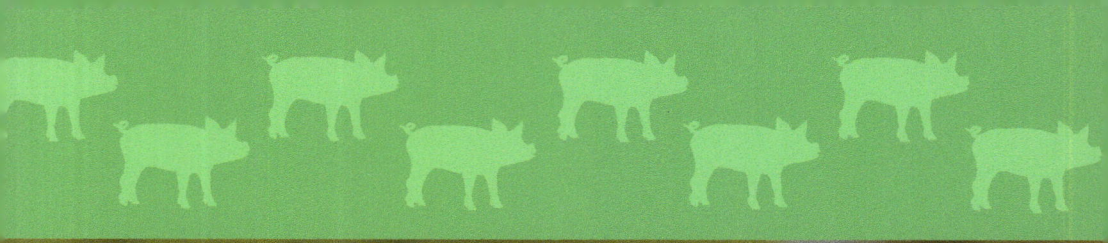

How Pigs Help Other Animals

Small bugs sometimes live on wild pigs. Bugs can be harmful to pigs if they bite or sting.

Birds called oxpeckers sit on the backs of wild pigs and eat the bugs. This helps the pigs and gives the birds lots of food to eat.

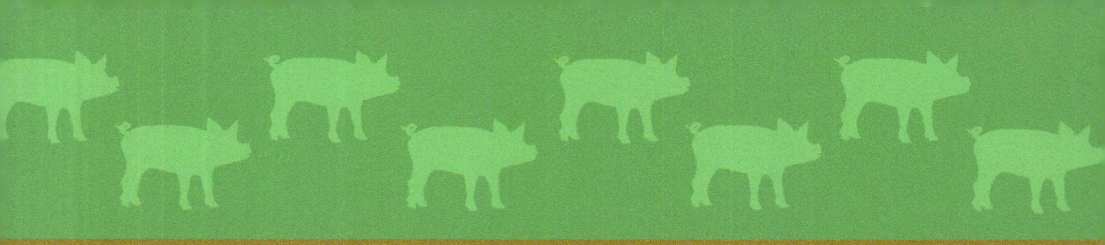

How Pigs Help Humans

Pigs are an important part of many people's diets. Many people would have less food to eat without pigs.

Some pigs have saved people's lives. They have been known to run for help if someone falls down, or warn their owners of a house fire.

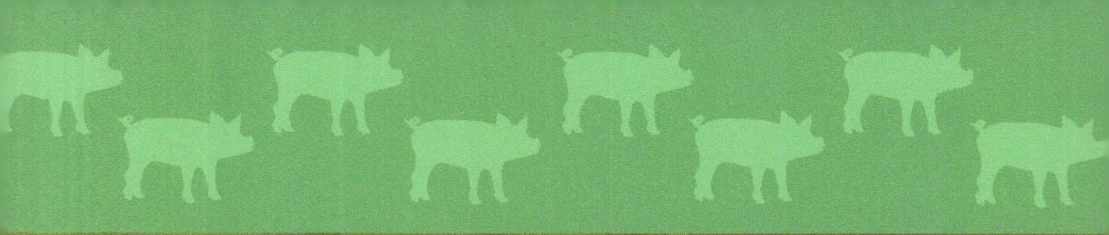

Pigs in Danger

Some pigs are endangered. This means there are very few of them left.

Visayan warty pigs live in the Philippines. The forests where they live are being destroyed by people. There are only a few hundred of them left.

How To Help Pigs

Pig meat is called pork. Many pigs that are raised for meat are kept in small cages.

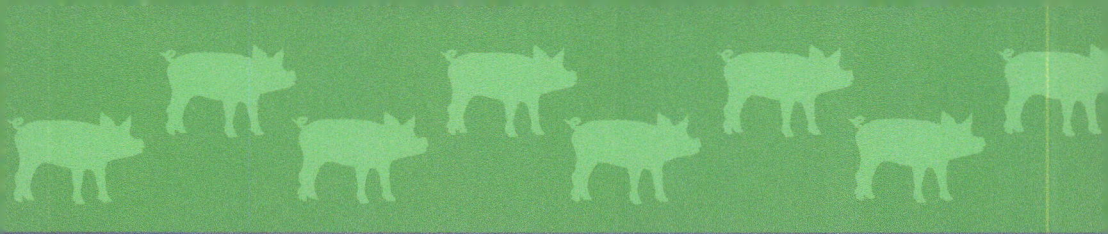

People are helping pigs by only buying pork products that are "free-range." This means the pigs were allowed outside.

Quiz

Test your knowledge of pigs by answering the following questions. The questions are based on what you have read in this book. The answers are listed on the bottom of the next page.

1 What do wild pigs eat?

2 What do pigs do when they are happy?

3 How old are pigs when they stop growing?

4 How many toes do pigs have?

5 How many pigs are kept by people?

6 How do pigs dig up dirt?

Explore other books in the Animals That Make a Difference series.

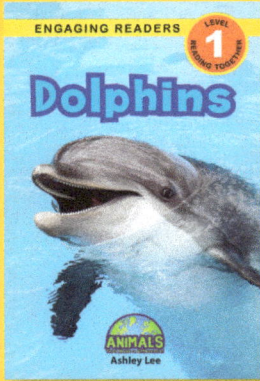

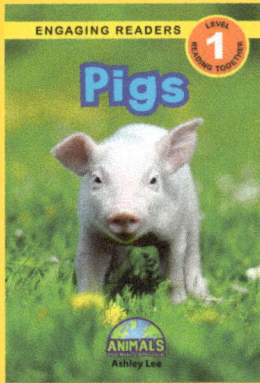

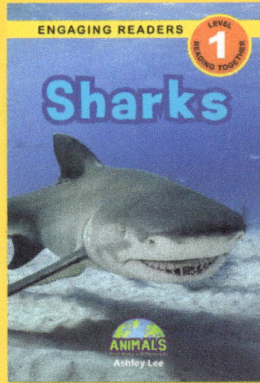

Bees

Bats

Birds

Dolphins

Horses

Lady Bugs

Pigs

Sharks

Squirrels

Visit www.engagebooks.com to explore more Engaging Readers.

Answers: 1. Leaves, roots, and grass 2. Wag their tails 3. Between 2 and 3 years old 4. Four 5. About 2 billion 6. With their noses

www.ingramcontent.com/pod-product-compliance
Lightning Source LLC
Chambersburg PA
CBHW051239020426
42331CB00016B/3443

www.ingramcontent.com/pod-product-compliance
Lightning Source LLC
Chambersburg PA
CBHW051239020426
42331CB00016B/3439